DR. MONIQUE BRUNER

By Faith Thou Art Healed

The Lord Loves you!
M Bruner

Copyright ©2022 by Dr. Monique Miles Bruner

All rights reserved. No part of this publication may be reproduced, distributed or transmitted in any form or by any means, without prior written permission.

Stellar Creative LLC
Oklahoma City, Oklahoma 73134
www.stellarcreates.com

By Faith Thou Art Healed / Dr. Monique Miles Bruner – 3rd ed.
ISBN 978-1-387-53038-0
Imprint: Lulu.com

Contents

Preface	iv
Your Words Are Important!	1
Cast Down Those Thoughts and Imaginations That Don't Line Up...	3
Long Life Belongs to You-Don't Give Up! Base Your Faith on...	7
Snap Out of That Depression, your Attitude Determines Your...	8
Use Your Authority & Resist Fear!	10
We have been redeemed out from under the bondage of sickness...	12
You Are an Overcomer Through Jesus Christ!	15
The Word of God Brings Healing	21
Make Jesus The Lord of Your Life, Reverence Him by Closing...	22
Know That When You Ask the Lord For Healing, It Is Already...	24
The Will of God Is His Blessing of Goodness That Is For you...	26

Preface

We suggest that you go over these Scriptures below a couple of times a day if you are in need of healing. Allow the Holy Spirit to impart faith into your heart as you read these Words of Life. Speak them out over yourself in the first person tense, laying claim to them by faith, with the understanding that they are your inheritance as a child of God.

Be sure and browse through our Healing Check List after reading through these powerful promises of healing; this will help you stay on track! This is very important: The Bible tells us in Romans 10:17 that faith comes by hearing and hearing by the Word of God.

Hebrews 7:25 *Because Jesus has become the guarantee of a better covenant (verse 22),* "Therefore He is also able to *save to the uttermost* those who come to God through Him, since He always lives to make intercession for them." Take a look at this scripture in the Amplified Version: "Therefore He is able also to save to the uttermost (completely, perfectly, finally, and for all time and eternity) those who come to God through Him, since He is always living to make petition to God and intercede with Him and intervene for them." NOTE - It is important to remember that the word "save" is the Greek word "Sozo" which literally means to heal, preserve, save, do well, be (make) whole. It means deliverance in the present as well as in the future or in eternity, physical as well as spiritual. Jesus used this word to denote healing of the body as well as forgiveness of sins. Always translate this word as "save - heal" when you come across it in the Word.

Acts 13:38-39 "Therefore let it be known to you, brethren, that through this

Man [Jesus] is preached to you the forgiveness of sins; and by Him everyone who believes is *justified* [declared righteous] from all things from which you could not be justified by the law of Moses." NOTE - From now on you need to train yourself to translate the word "justified" as declared righteous. That is the literal Greek translation. This will really help you when you read the book of Romans. You can remember it by: just-if-I'd never sinned. That is righteousness - to be in right standing with God. 2 Corinthians 5:7 tells us plainly that as born-again believer's we have become the righteousness of God in Christ. Because of the forgiveness of sins, through His shed blood, we are redeemed and declared righteous from ALL THINGS which we could not be declared righteous from apart from His redemptive work.

Romans 8:11 "But if the Spirit of Him who raised Jesus from the dead dwells in you, He who raised Christ from the dead will also give life to your mortal (*Natural, Earthly*) bodies through His Spirit who dwells in you." NOTE - Take a close look at this Scripture, this is talking about your body that you have now, not the one you're going to receive one day in heaven! Allow the Lord to impart His life into you by placing faith in His Word. Begin to praise Him for this promise.

2 Corinthians 4:10-11 "Always bearing about in the body the dying of the Lord Jesus (which was for our victory), that the life also of Jesus might be made manifest in our body. For we which live are always delivered unto death for Jesus' sake, that the life also of Jesus might be made manifest in our mortal flesh." - *Bodily Health!!!*

Matthew 6:9-10 "Our Father in heaven, hallowed be your name. Your kingdom come. Your will be done on Earth as it is in heaven."

NOTE - Jesus always prays the will of God, and He prays that the will of God be done here on the earth just as it is in heaven. People in heaven are not sick, so we can clearly see it is God's will that we also be free from sickness and disease.

Journal

Your Words Are Important!

Isaiah 57:19 "I create the fruit of the lips; Peace, peace to him that is far off, and to him that is near, saith the LORD; and I will heal him." NOTE - The word "fruit" here means produce. God creates what you produce from your mouth when we believe and speak the Word of God

Mark 11:22-23 "And Jesus answering saith unto them, Have faith in God. For verily I say unto you, That whosoever shall say unto this mountain, Be thou removed, and be thou cast into the sea; and shall not doubt in his heart, but shall believe that those things which he saith shall come to pass; he shall have whatsoever he saith." NOTE - What kind of mountains or obstacles do you have in your life right now? Obey Jesus and command that mountain of pain, cancer, disease, to go *now* out of your body in the Name of Jesus. Jesus said you can have what you say. Begin to call your body whole, healed, well - don't stop, don't listen to your body, don't listen to doubt and fear, listen to Jesus, listen to His Word!

Job 22:26-28 "For then you will delight in the Almighty and lift up your face to God. You will pray to Him, and He will hear you; and you will pay your vows. "You will also decree a thing, and it will be established for you; and light will shine on your ways." NOTE - Give voice to the promises in the Word, and lay claim to them as your inheritance. Decree that you are healed!

"Lord, you said that by your stripes I am healed, so on the authority of Your Word, I decree that I am healed and that sickness and disease have no hold on me, and they

must go in the Name of Jesus!"

Remember To Give Testimony Of Your Healing!

Revelation 12:11 "And they overcame him by the blood of the Lamb, and by the word of their testimony…" NOTE - When your healing manifests itself, and you recover and have the opportunity to testify to the grace of the Lord - Do it!!! The Lord wants you to give glory to Him for what He has done, and it will also serve to help build faith in someone else who has a need.

Deuteronomy 30:19-20 "I call heaven and earth as witnesses today against you, that I have set before you life and death, blessing and cursing; *therefore choose life*, that both you and your descendants may live; that you may love the LORD your God, that you may obey His voice, and that you may cling to Him, for He is your life and the length of your days; and that you may dwell in the land which the LORD swore to your fathers, to Abraham, Isaac, and Jacob, to give them." NOTE - Just as it was when this was spoken to the children of Israel, it is true for us today - we need to make up our minds and choose life - it is there for us. Fall in love with Jesus, fall in love with the Word, health and life will be a natural result!

Job 5:26 "You shall come to the grave at a full age, as a sheaf of grain ripens in its season."

Psalm 91:16 "With long life I will satisfy him, and show him My salvation." NOTE - Here God is saying live until you're satisfied!

Psalm 118:17 "I shall not die, but live, and declare the works of the LORD." NOTE - Agree with this right now! Declare it with your voice! God has a plan for your life here on the Earth.

Journal

Cast Down Those Thoughts and Imaginations That Don't Line Up With The Word of God!

2 Corinthians 10:4-5 "(For the weapons of our warfare are not carnal, but mighty through God to the pulling down of strong holds;) Casting down imaginations, and every high thing that exalteth itself against the knowledge of God, and bringing into captivity every thought to the obedience of Christ" NOTE - Keep your focus on the promises of God, you have to make yourself stay focused.

Isaiah 43:25-26 "I, even I, am He who blots out your transgressions for My own sake; and I will not remember your sins. Put Me in remembrance; let us contend together; state your case, that you may be acquitted." NOTE - Your case was settled when Jesus went to the cross in your behalf!

If you have accepted Jesus Christ as Lord, then,

"It is finished!!!"

Mark 16:17-18 "And these signs shall follow them that believe; In my name . . . they shall lay hands on the sick, and they shall recover." NOTE - Find someone who believes God's Word regarding healing and have them lay hands on you and pray for you in faith believing. James 5:16 says "that the effectual fervent prayer of a righteous man avails much."

Isaiah 40:31 "But they that wait upon the Lord shall renew their strength; they shall mount up with wings as eagles; they shall run, and not be weary, and they shall walk and not faint." NOTE - The word "wait" in this verse implies a positive action of hope, based on knowing that the Word of God is a true fact and that it will soon come to pass - waiting with earnest expectation!

Psalm 34:19 "Many are the afflictions of the righteous, but the LORD delivers him out of them all."

Jeremiah 30:17 "For I will restore health unto you, and I will heal you of your wounds, saith the Lord."

Isaiah 53:4-5 "Surely He hath borne our grief's (Lit. sicknesses) and carried our sorrows (Lit. pains) yet we did esteem Him stricken, smitten of God and afflicted. But He was wounded for our transgressions, He was bruised for our iniquities; the chastisement of our peace was upon Him; and by His stripes we are healed." NOTE - The last part of this verse, *"by His stripes we are healed,"* is not talking about spiritual healing, as some have taught, but definite physical healing. God does not "heal" a human spirit, he recreates it. He does however, heal our bodies and minds. This clearly shows that your healing was paid for at the cross!

Jeremiah 33:6 "Behold, I will bring you health and cure, and I will cure you, and will reveal unto you the abundance of peace and truth."

Matthew 18:19 "Again I say to you that if two of you agree on Earth concerning anything that they ask, it will be done for them by My Father in heaven." NOTE - The prayer of agreement is powerful - have someone agree with you for your healing!

Mark 11:24 "Therefore I say to you whatever things you ask when you pray, believe that you receive them, and you will have them." *Surely this includes healing!*

Isaiah 58:8 "Thy light shall break forth as the morning, and thy health shall spring forth speedily; and thy righteousness shall go before thee: the glory of the Lord shall be thy rear guard."

Psalm 41:3 (Amplified Version) "The Lord will sustain, refresh, and strengthen him on his bed of languishing; *all his bed* You [O Lord] will turn, change, and transform in his illness." The phrase "all his bed" in the Hebrew has the meaning of; all that he is afflicted with, or all of his condition that he is lying with" It is always His will to turn, change and transform our mourning into dancing - Psalm 30:11

Isaiah 53:4-5 "Surely He hath borne our grief's (Lit. sicknesses) and carried our sorrows (Lit. pains) yet we did esteem Him stricken, smitten of God and afflicted. But He was wounded for our transgressions, He was bruised for our iniquities; the chastisement of our peace was upon Him; and by His stripes we are healed."

NOTE - The last part of this verse, *"by His stripes we are healed,"* is not talking about spiritual healing, as some have taught, but definite physical healing. God does not "heal" a human spirit; he recreates it. He does however, heal our bodies and minds. This clearly shows that your healing was paid for at the cross!

Jeremiah 33:6 "Behold, I will bring you health and cure, and I will cure you, and will reveal unto you the abundance of peace and truth."

Matthew 18:19 "Again I say to you that if two of you agree on Earth concerning anything that they ask, it will be done for them by My Father in heaven." NOTE - The prayer of agreement is powerful - have someone agree with you for your healing!

Mark 11:24 "Therefore I say to you whatever things you ask when you pray, believe that you receive them, and you will have them." *Surely this includes* *healing!*

Isaiah 58:8 "Thy light shall break forth as the morning, and thy health shall spring forth speedily; and thy righteousness shall go before thee: the glory of the Lord shall be thy rear guard."

Psalm 41:3 *(Amplified Version)* "The Lord will sustain, refresh, and strengthen him on his bed of languishing; *all his bed* You [O Lord] will turn, change, and transform in his illness." The phrase "all his bed" in the Hebrew has the meaning of; all that he is afflicted with, or all of his condition that he is lying with" It is always His will to turn, change and transform our mourning into dancing - Psalm 30:11

Hebrews 10:35-36 "Therefore do not cast away your confidence, which has great reward. For you have need of endurance, so that after you have done the will of God, you may receive the promise." NOTE - Remember that the will of God is the Word of God!

Journal

Long Life Belongs to You-Don't Give Up! Base Your Faith on The Promises of God!

Genesis 6:3 And the LORD said, "My Spirit shall not strive with man forever, for he is indeed flesh; yet his days shall be one hundred and twenty years." NOTE - Did you see it! The promise of God is that you live a good long life, even to 120 if you so desire. Speak to that mountain of death and command it to be removed. Begin to grab hold of this promise of long life and lay claim to it with your spoken words.

Psalm 90:10 "The days of our lives are seventy years; and if by reason of strength they are eighty years, yet their boast is only labor and sorrow; for it is soon cut off, and we fly away." NOTE - Many take this verse to be the cap that God has set for mankind's lifespan upon the earth. However, this psalm was written by Moses and this verse pertains to the disobedient children of Israel that came out of Egypt being led by Moses who, because of their unbelief, were condemned to live out their lives wondering in the desert until each one had died. Only their children, and Moses, Joshua and Caleb would enter into the Promised Land. Moses went on to live 120 years and the scripture says that his strength had not departed him and his eyes were not dim. He also was very able to climb the mountain God had commanded him to climb where he died. Joshua and Caleb also lived to be over 100.

Journal

Snap Out of That Depression, your Attitude Determines Your Altitude!

Hebrews 12:12-13 "Wherefore lift up the hands which hang down, and the feeble knees; And make straight paths for your feet, lest that which is lame be turned out of the way; but let it rather be healed."

Psalm 42:11 "Why art thou cast down, O my soul? and why art thou disquieted within me? Hope thou in God: for I shall yet praise him, who is the health of my countenance, and my God." **We Can Have Confidence In Him, For God Cannot Lie!**

Hebrews 10:23 "Let us hold fast the profession of our faith without wavering; (for he is faithful that promised)" NOTE - Remember Hebrews 6:18 says that it is impossible for God to lie!

I John 5:14-15 "Now this is the confidence that we have in Him, that if we ask anything according to His will, He hears us. And if we know that He hears us, whatever we ask, we know that we have the petitions that we have asked of Him." NOTE - It's easy to know the will of God. The Word of God is the will of God! Jeremiah 1:12 says that He watches over His Word to perform it.

wholly; and I pray God your whole spirit and soul and body be preserved blameless [sound, complete and intact] unto the coming of our Lord Jesus Christ." NOTE - It is very clear in this passage that wholeness, wellness, and health is for the complete make-up of man, spiritual, mental, and physical.

1 Peter 2:24 "Who Himself bore our sins in His own body on the tree, that we, having died to sins, might live for righteousness— by whose stripes you were healed." NOTE - Past tense *"You were healed".* Jesus paid it all for your total deliverance - spirit, soul and body!

Psalm 103:2-3 "Bless the Lord, O my soul, and forget not all His benefits: Who forgiveth all thine iniquities; who heals all thy diseases" NOTE - Notice it doesn't say some, it says all! It also states that healing is one of the benefits that belongs to the believer along with the benefit of having our sin forgiven.

3 John 2 "Beloved, I wish above all things that thou mayest prosper and be in health, even as thy soul prospereth."

Jeremiah 17:14 "Heal me, O LORD, and I shall be healed; save me, and I shall be saved: for thou art my praise." NOTE - Once a person finally sees that healing is a finished work along with salvation, paid for at the same time with the same healing Blood, then you can get excited about this verse saying; "you did it Lord for me, then according to this verse I will agree and say I will have healing just as I have salvation, it's mine NOW!"

James 5:14-15 "Is any sick among you? Let him call for the elders of the church; and let them pray over him, anointing him with oil in the name of the Lord: And the prayer of faith shall save the sick, and the Lord shall raise him up; and if he have committed sins, they shall be forgiven him."

Journal

Use Your Authority & Resist Fear!

Matthew 18:18 "Verily I say unto you, whatsoever you shall bind on earth shall be bound in heaven: and whatsoever you shall loose on earth shall be loosed in heaven." NOTE - The word "bind" means to forbid, the word "loose" means to let go or to allow to go free. Do not allow sickness, pain or disease run free in your body, bind it or forbid it to stay there any longer because of your rights as a believer. Put your foot down and command it to leave in the Name of Jesus!!!

John 10:10 "The thief (Satan) does not come except to steal, and to kill, and to destroy. I (Jesus) have come that they may have life, and that they may have it more abundantly." NOTE - Here we see the desired will of the Lord for every believer, that we experience abundant life. According to this verse, He came for this very purpose. We also see clearly that it is not God who afflicts us. The word here for life is the Greek word "Zoe." Sickness and disease are truly not in His plan for us, simply because He has none to give.

Luke 10:19 "Behold, I give unto you power (authority) to tread on serpents and scorpions, and over all the power of the enemy: and nothing shall by any means hurt you." NOTE - This is an exciting verse as Jesus said He has given us authoritative power over ALL, not some of the enemy! Command Satan to take his hands off of you. Command sickness and disease to leave you now in the Name of Jesus.

Isaiah 41:10 "So do not fear, for I am with you; do not be dismayed, for I am your God. I will strengthen you and help you; I will uphold you with my righteous right hand."

Isaiah 54:17 "No weapon formed against you shall prosper, and every tongue which rises against you in judgment YOU shall condemn. This is the heritage (birthright) of the servants of the LORD, and their righteousness is from Me," says the LORD." NOTE - Sickness is judging you falsely; it is your birthright to live in health. You condemn it, with the Word of God, and command it to leave your body.

Journal

We have been redeemed out from under the bondage of sickness and disease!

Galatians 3:13-14 "Christ hath redeemed us from the curse of the law, being made a curse for us; for it is written, Cursed is every one that hangeth on a tree: That the blessings of Abraham might come on the Gentiles through Jesus Christ." NOTE - The curse of the law includes sickness and disease and is found in Deuteronomy 28:15-68. The first 14 verses of the chapter pertain to the blessing, and the rest of the chapter describes the curse! By the shed Blood of Jesus Christ we were purchased out of or out from under the curse!!! Especially look at verse 61, it states all sickness and all disease in the world, even those not written in the Book, so therefore *we are redeemed from it all!!!*

Proverbs 26:2 "Like a flitting sparrow, like a flying swallow, so a curse without cause shall not alight." NOTE - As we continue in Christ, the curse has no right to take root in our lives.

Romans 8:2 "For the law of the Spirit of life in Christ Jesus has made me free from the law of sin and death." *And the effects of death and the curse!*

Colossians 1:13 "He has delivered us from the power of darkness and conveyed us into the kingdom of the Son of His love" NOTE - Remember there is no sickness or disease in the kingdom of God! Here again is another wonderful scripture proving your birthright of healing.

John 15:7 "If you abide in Me, and My words abide in you, you will ask what you desire, and it shall be done for you."

Isaiah 55:11 "So shall my word be that goeth forth out of my mouth: it shall not return unto me void, but it shall accomplish that which I please, and it shall prosper in the thing whereto I sent it."

Jeremiah 1:12 ".... I am alert and active watching over My Word to perform it." *Amplified* NOTE - God is looking, searching eagerly for someone to take Him at His Word so that He can perform it on their behalf.

Joshua 21:45 "Not a word failed of any good thing which the LORD had spoken to the house of Israel. All came to pass." **Healing is a good gift from God!**

James 1:17 "Every good gift and every perfect gift is from above, and cometh down from the Father of lights, with whom is no variableness, neither shadow of turning."

1 Corinthians 3:21-22 "Therefore let no one boast in men. For all things are yours: whether Paul or Apollos or Cephas, or the world or life or death, or things present or things to come—all are yours." NOTE - This says it so clear, the Lord is holding nothing back from us. Surely healing is included in the claim of "all things" and certainly is included in the word "life."

Romans 11:29 "For the gifts and the calling of God are irrevocable."

Philippians 2:13 "For it is God who works in you both to will and to do for his good pleasure."

Matthew 11:28 *(Amplified Version)* "Come to Me, all you who labor and are heavy-laden and overburdened, and I will cause you to rest. [I will ease and relieve and refresh your souls.]" NOTE - The word 'rest' here literally means to cease from toil or labor in order to recover and collect his strength, and implies a feeling of wholeness and well being. Place your focus onto Jesus and all that He has purchased for you. You are highly favored by God - He's given it all to you. Spend time each day just loving on God.

1 John 3:8b "For this purpose the Son of God was manifested, that He might destroy the works of the devil." Take a look at this same verse in the Amplified version - "The reason the Son of God was made manifest (visible) was to undo (destroy, loosen, and dissolve) the works the devil [has done]." NOTE -There is no doubt that sickness and disease are works of the devil, introduced to mankind through the fall as part of the curse. This Scripture is very clear that Jesus came to undo the works of the devil. Be assured that He accomplished His task- further proof that sickness and disease have no legal right to remain in your body as a child of God!

Command it to go in Jesus Name!

Journal

You Are an Overcomer Through Jesus Christ!

1 John 4:4 ". . . . greater is he that is in you, than he that is in the world."

1 John 5:4 "For whatsoever is born of God overcometh the world: and this is the victory that overcometh the world, even our faith." NOTE - In John 17:14 Jesus states that we as believer's are not of the world. Sickness, disease and failure belong to the world. As a believer, we are given the right to overcome that which comes against us by holding fast to the Word of God. While we do not deny that the problem or circumstance exists, we do however deny it the right to stay through our faith in God and His Word!!! Know this: Faith in God is victory all of the time!!!

Romans 8:31 "What shall we then say to these things? If God be for us, who can be against us" NOTE - You are a winner, you are victorious through the Lord Jesus Christ. Begin to see yourself the way God sees you.

1 John 4:17 " Love has been perfected among us in this: that we may have boldness in the day of judgment; because as He is, so are we in this world." NOTE - Not only can we have boldness in the day of judgment, but we can have boldness now in this life in the face of adversity, knowing who we are in Christ, knowing what belongs to us in Him and tenaciously holding onto it, refusing what the enemy wants us to have. Insist on having the blessing of the Lord manifested in you - praise Him for it now, worship Him!!!

1 Corinthians 5:15-17 "Do you not know that your bodies are members of Christ? Shall I then take the members of Christ and make them members of a harlot? Certainly not! Or do you not know that he who is joined to a harlot is one body with her? For "the two," He says, "shall become one flesh." But he who is joined to the Lord is one spirit with Him." NOTE - Sickness has no right to Him, so it has no legal right to us. It is illegal, off limits, it has no right to stay. Take a firm stand and run off the attack and lie of the enemy. You belong to Him, you are washed in His precious Blood, the covenant Blood.

2 Peter 1:3-4 "As His divine power has given to us all things that pertain to life and godliness, through the knowledge of Him who called us by glory and virtue, by which have been given to us exceedingly great and precious promises, that through these you may be partakers of the divine nature, having escaped the corruption that is in the world through lust." NOTE - Notice the past tense use of "has" given us all things that pertain to life!!! The blessing of health was purchased for us at the cross, it belongs to you now. Notice the importance of the Word of God, your healing must be rooted steadfastly on the Word, not on what you see or how you feel.

1 Corinthians 1:9 "God is faithful, by whom you were called into the fellowship of His Son, Jesus Christ our Lord." NOTE The word "fellowship" is a strong covenant word in the original Greek text. It means: intimacy, partnership and participation, and also communion. Know that He is life, the purest form of life, and He's called us to share intimately in it with Him.

Romans 5:17 "For if by the one man's offense [Adam] death reigned through the one, much more those who receive abundance of grace and of the gift of righteousness *will reign in life* through the one, Jesus Christ." NOTE - Did you notice, it did not say you might or you possibly could, it says you *will* reign in life (this life in the here and now). Are you reigning in life or are you being rained on? If you are not experiencing victory, know that it is a breech of the Word of God for it to remain and become the norm. Get mad, with a righteous indignation, and command the circumstances to leave and take hold of the victory that is yours through the Word. For this is the will of God!

Genesis 1:28 "And God blessed them, and God said unto them, Be fruitful, and multiply, and replenish the earth, and subdue it: and have dominion over the fish of the sea, and over the fowl of the air, and over every living thing that moveth upon the earth." NOTE - The red blood cells of your body already obey this verse, as they are being multiplied and replenished every 80 - 120 days! Look at the rest of what God said to mankind subdue and have dominion… over every living thing! Wow!

Proverbs 4:20-22 "My Son, attend to My words; incline thine ear unto My sayings. Let them not depart from thine eyes; keep them in the midst of thine heart. For they are life unto those that find them, and health (Lit. medicine) to all their flesh." NOTE Here it is as plain as it can be: the taking of God's Word is life and medicine to your flesh. So just don't take your prescribed natural medicine alone, add the Word of God along with it. Prescribed medicine can heal and help some things, but God's medicine can heal all.

John 8:32 "And ye shall know the truth, and the truth shall make you free." NOTE - The Word of God is truth see John 17:17. Once you know the truth concerning healing in God's redemptive plan, then you can begin to exercise faith and expect the promises of God to manifest in you - and they will - REJOICE!!!

Jeremiah 23:29 "Is not My word like a fire? says the LORD, And like a hammer that breaks the rock in pieces?" NOTE - The Word of God *IS* an all consuming fire that will melt away and burn off that which is not of God, and a powerful crushing force to break apart even the toughest and most stubborn circumstances. Continue taking the hammer of God's Word and continue to hit the situations in your life that are not of God, until they give way and become as the Word says they should be. Persistence breaks down resistance!

2 Timothy 3:16-17 "All Scripture is given by inspiration of God, and is profitable for doctrine, for reproof, for correction, for instruction in righteousness, that the man of God may be complete, thoroughly equipped for every good work." NOTE - Does your body and or mind need correction? God's Word is just the medicine. If you are sick you cannot do the work of the ministry- know that God wants you to be able bodied, a living example in every area of His grace and mercy and power.

John 6:63 "It is the Spirit who gives life; the flesh profits nothing. The words that I speak to you are spirit, and they are life." NOTE - God's Word is healing, it will bring health to your flesh.

See Proverbs 4:22.

Proverbs 4:20-22 "My Son, attend to My words; incline thine ear unto My sayings. Let them not depart from thine eyes; keep them in the midst of thine heart. For they are life unto those that find them, and health (Lit. medicine) to all their flesh." NOTE Here it is as plain as it can be: the taking of God's Word is life and medicine to your flesh. So just don't take your prescribed natural medicine alone, add the Word of God along with it. Prescribed medicine can heal and help some things, but God's medicine can heal all.

John 8:32 "And ye shall know the truth, and the truth shall make you free." NOTE - The Word of God is truth see John 17:17. Once you know the truth concerning healing in God's redemptive plan, then you can begin to exercise faith and expect the promises of God to manifest in you - and they will - REJOICE!!!

Jeremiah 23:29 "Is not My word like a fire? says the LORD, And like a hammer that breaks the rock in pieces?" NOTE - The Word of God *IS* an all consuming fire that will melt away and burn off that which is not of God, and a powerful crushing force to break apart even the toughest and most stubborn circumstances. Continue taking the hammer of God's Word and continue to hit the situations in your life that are not of God, until they give way and become as the Word says they should be. Persistence breaks down resistance!

Timothy 3:16-17 "All Scripture is given by inspiration of God, and is profitable for doctrine, for reproof, for correction, for instruction in righteousness, that the man of God may be complete, thoroughly equipped for every good work."

NOTE - Does your body and or mind need correction? God's Word is just the medicine. If you are sick you cannot do the work of the ministry- know that God wants you to be able bodied, a living example in every area of His grace and mercy and power.

John 6:63 "It is the Spirit who gives life; the flesh profits nothing. The words that I speak to you are spirit, and they are life." NOTE - God's Word is healing, it will bring health to your flesh.

Psalm 121:7-8 "The Lord shall preserve (keep) you from all evil; He shall preserve your soul (life). The Lord shall preserve your going out and your coming in from this time forth and even forevermore." NOTE - Notice He said He would keep or preserve us from all evil. This surely includes sickness and disease. The word for preserve means to guard, keep, to hedge about, to protect, to attend to. Praise the Lord! His promise is to do this now and forevermore. Begin to thank Him and praise Him for it.

Hebrews 13:20-21 *(Amplified Version)* "Now may the God of peace [Who is the Author and the Giver of peace], Who brought again from among the dead our Lord Jesus, that great Shepherd of the sheep, by the blood [that sealed, ratified] the everlasting agreement (covenant, testament), strengthen (complete, perfect) *and make you what you ought to be* and equip you with everything good that you may carry out His will; [while He Himself] works in you and accomplishes that which is pleasing in His sight, through Jesus

Christ (the Messiah); to Whom be the glory forever and ever (to the ages of the ages). Amen (so be it).

NOTE: The author of Hebrews is praying a blessing in accordance with the will of God for completeness and wholeness which is intended through the Blood Covenant. May you be strengthened, be made complete and be perfected, be made *what you ought to be* (because of the shed Blood) and equipped with everything good so you can accomplish His will! Wow!

Journal

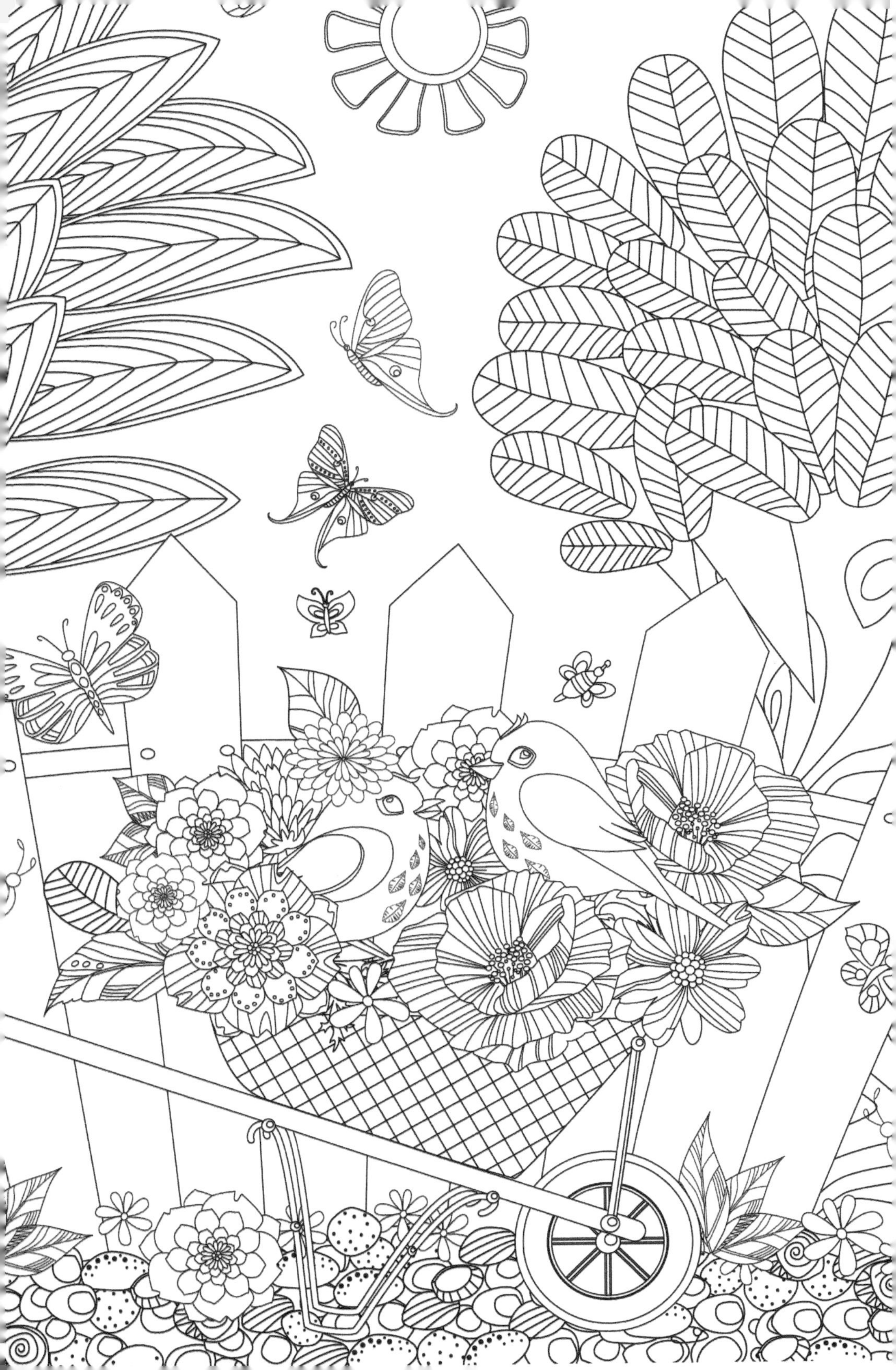

The Word of God Brings Healing

Psalm 119:50 "This is my comfort in my affliction, for your Word has given my life."

Romans 10:17 "So then faith comes by hearing and hearing by the word of God." NOTE - Faith for healing comes by hearing God's Word concerning healing. So just as you may be taking medicine two or three times a day, do the same thing with the promises in the Word of God regarding healing, and allow your faith to be built up! You'll be amazed at the change that will take place. This includes cancer, bacteria, parasites, viruses and all microorganisms that cause sickness and disease. He gave the blessing, He gave the command, He gave *you* the right - now do it.

Colossians 1:13 "He has delivered us from the power of darkness and conveyed us into the kingdom of the Son of His love" NOTE - To be conveyed is to be transferred, removed out of one and placed into another. The power of darkness, which includes the curse, no longer has a hold on us as we are now members of a different kingdom - the kingdom of God.

Make Jesus The Lord of Your Life, Reverence Him by Closing All Doors To The Enemy, Giving Him First Place!

Proverbs 3:7-8 "Do not be wise in your own eyes; fear the LORD and depart from evil. It will be health to your flesh, and strength to your bones." NOTE - The term "fear the Lord" means to reverence and worship the Lord in all things.

Exodus 15:26 "If thou will diligently harken to the voice of the Lord thy God, and wilt do that which is right in His sight, and wilt give ear to His commandments, and keep all His statutes, I will put (permit) none of these diseases upon thee, which I have brought upon the Egyptians: for I am the Lord that healeth thee."

Exodus 23:25 "So you shall serve (worship) the Lord your God and He will bless your bread and your water. And I will take sickness away from the midst of you." NOTE - True worship from the heart is a key to walking in divine health. Humbleness of heart. Close every door to the devil that you are aware of. Take time each day to worship and love on God from your heart.

Psalm 91:9-10 "Because thou hast made the LORD, which is my refuge, even the Most High, thy habitation; There shall no evil befall thee, neither shall any plague come nigh thy dwelling."

Psalm 121:7-8 "The Lord shall preserve (keep) you from all evil; He shall preserve your soul (life). The Lord shall preserve your going out and your coming in from this time forth and even forevermore." NOTE - Notice He said He would keep or preserve us from all evil. This surely includes sickness and disease. The word for preserve means to guard, keep, to hedge about, to protect, to attend to. Praise the Lord! His promise is to do this now and forevermore. Begin to thank Him and praise Him for it.

Hebrews 13:20-21 *(Amplified Version)* "Now may the God of peace [Who is the Author and the Giver of peace], Who brought again from among the dead our Lord Jesus, that great Shepherd of the sheep, by the blood [that sealed, ratified] the everlasting agreement (covenant, testament), strengthen (complete, perfect) *and make you what you ought to be* and equip you with everything good that you may carry out His will; [while He Himself] works in you and accomplishes that which is pleasing in His sight, through Jesus Christ (the Messiah); to Whom be the glory forever and ever (to the ages of the ages). Amen (so be it). NOTE The author of Hebrews is praying a blessing in accordance with the will of God for completeness and wholeness which is intended through the Blood Covenant. May you be strengthened, be made complete and be perfected, be made *what you ought to be* (because of the shed Blood) and equipped with everything good, so you can accomplish His will! Wow!

Malachi 4:2-3 "But unto you that fear (reverence, worship) My name shall the Sun of Righteousness arise with healing in His wings; and you shall go forth, and grow up as calves of the stall. "You shall trample the wicked for they shall be ashes under the soles of your feet on the day that I do this, says the Lord of hosts" NOTE - I love this verse! This verse is a great promise and even tells us when it became a reality for us. "On the day that I do this" was at Calvary. Now the enemy is "ashes" under our feet and healing and protection belong to us. See Luke 10:19 also.

Journal

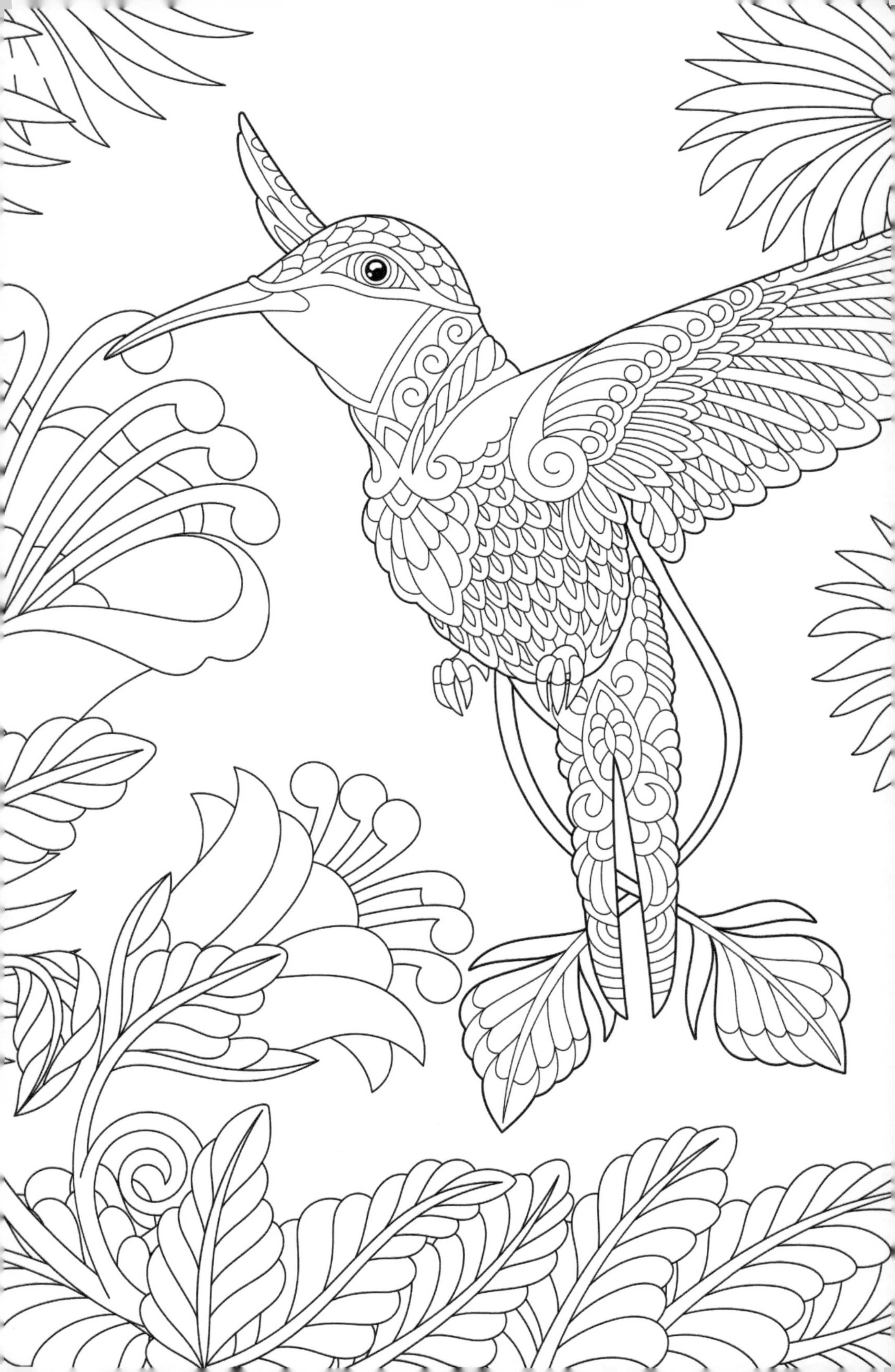

Know That When You Ask the Lord For Healing, It Is Already His Will And He Hears You And He Agrees. Know He Has Already Settled It In The Atonement Of the Blood of Jesus Christ – He Says "Yes"!

Psalm 30:2 "O LORD my God, I cried unto thee, and thou hast healed me."

Psalm 107:19-20 "Then they cry unto the LORD in their trouble, and he saveth them out of their distresses. He sent his word, and healed them, and delivered them from their destructions."

Matthew 7:7-8 "Ask, and it will be given to you; seek, and you will find; knock, and it will be opened to you. "For everyone who asks receives, and he who seeks finds, and to him who knocks it will be opened." NOTE - The word "ask" in the Greek has the meaning of insistent asking with a knowing of what belongs to the one making the request. Presenting a solid requisition to God, knowing He longs to distribute what He has to the one in need. Look at James 1:5-8 we must ask in faith, and faith always knows, it never wishes!

I John 5:14-15 "Now this is the confidence that we have in Him, that if we ask anything according to His will, He hears us. And if we know that He hears us, whatever we ask, we know that we have the petitions that we have asked of Him." NOTE - The Word of God is the will of God. If you see it in the Word of God then you can be assured that it is the will of God. The Lord is not trying to keep healing from you, He is trying to get it to you *Just Believe!*

2 Corinthians 1:20 "For all the promises of God in Him are Yes, and in Him Amen, to the glory of God through us." NOTE Notice that according to God all of His promises towards us are "YES" and amen (so be it!) or it is settled! There aren't any "no's" from the Lord toward us when it comes to performing His Word in our behalf. -Now *that's good news!*

Psalm 35:27 "Let them shout for joy and be glad, Who favor my righteous cause; And let them say continually, "Let the LORD be magnified, Who has pleasure in the prosperity of His servant." NOTE - The word in the Hebrew for prosperity here is *"shalom"* and we know it as the word for peace. However, in the Hebrew this word literally means health, prosperity and peace, wholeness, welfare. So you can clearly see the mind of God who takes pleasure in the health, wholeness, prosperity and peace of we, His children! Once you get a hold of this, praise and adoration will naturally flow forth in pure appreciation for who He is to us and all that He has already done for us. Fear and doubt will no longer have a place in your thinking. What an awesome God He is!!!

Journal

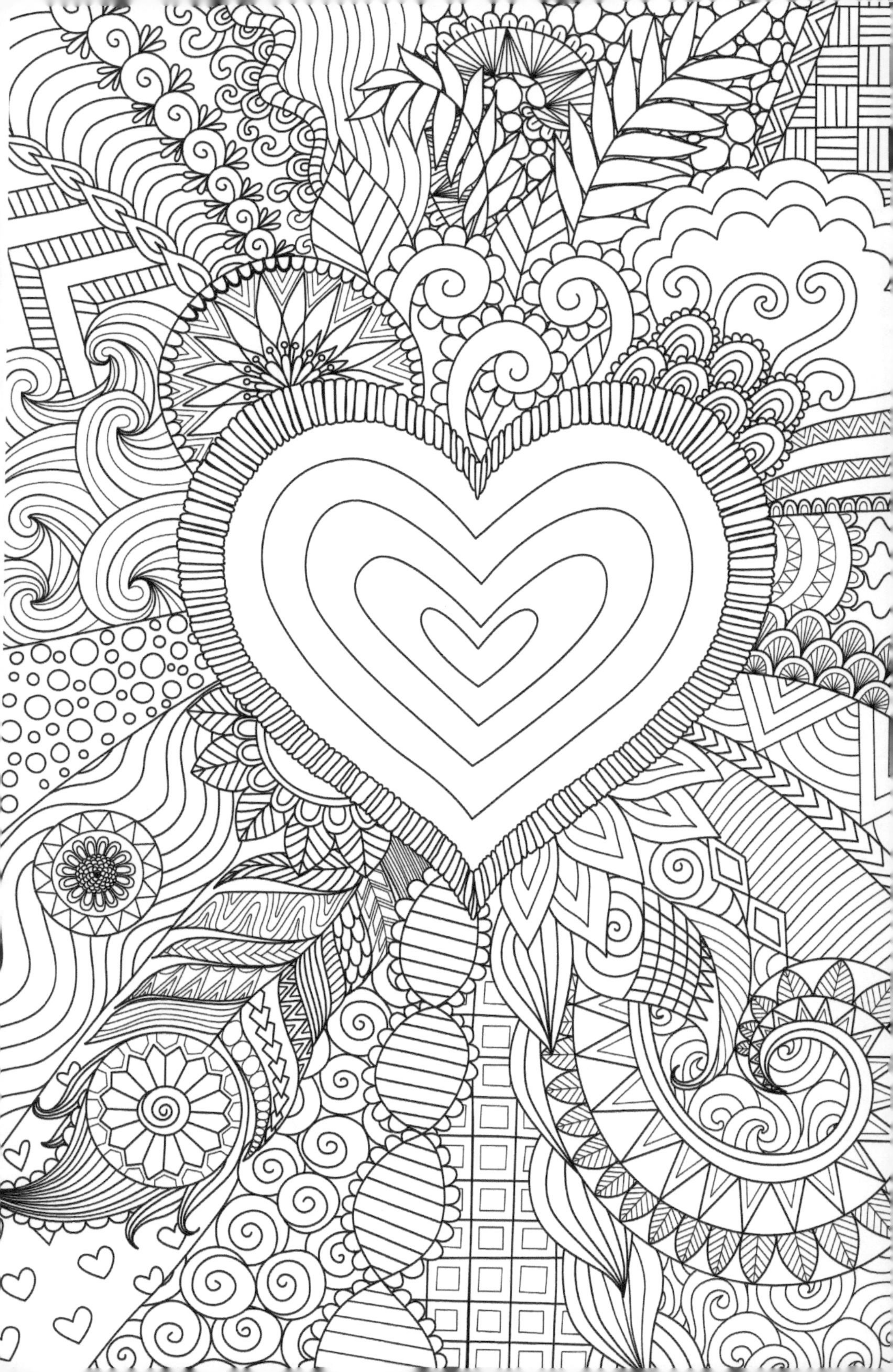

The Will of God Is His Blessing of Goodness That Is For you Now!

Jeremiah 29:11 "For I know the thoughts that I think toward you, says the Lord, thoughts of peace and not of evil, to give you a future and a hope (an expected end)." NOTE - The word for peace here in the Hebrew is the word *shalom* and implies the meaning of health and prosperity, which is obviously His will as it is the end or goal that the Lord is expecting for us. Begin to expect it also - yes, that's right - get your hopes way up!

Luke 12:32 "Do not fear, little flock, for it is your Father's good pleasure to give you the kingdom." NOTE - Along with the kingdom, come all the Kingdom blessings and benefits! Realize it gives God pleasure to give to you, He is a giver - He is love and love gives. So cast of fear, and put a smile on your face - you are rich in Him. Just receive it.

Journal

Journal

Journal

Journal

Journal

Journal

Journal

Journal

Journal

Journal

Journal

Journal

Journal

Journal

Journal

Journal

Journal

Journal

Journal

Journal

Journal